The Tao of Politics
Anthology

The Tao of George W. Bush was published in 2003
The Tao of Red States and Blue States was published in 2005
The Tao of Politics was published in 2005
The Tao of America appears here for the first time

The Tao of Politics Anthology

Ed Bremson

iUniverse, Inc.

New York Lincoln Shanghai

The Tao of Politics Anthology

Copyright © 2006 by Thomas E. Bremson

iUniverse books may be ordered through booksellers or by contacting:

iUniverse
2021 Pine Lake Road, Suite 100
Lincoln, NE 68512
www.iuniverse.com
1-800-Authors (1-800-288-4677)

ISBN-13: 978-0-595-38473-0 (pbk)
ISBN-13: 978-0-595-82854-8 (ebk)
ISBN-10: 0-595-38473-0 (pbk)
ISBN-10: 0-595-82854-X (ebk)

Printed in the United States of America

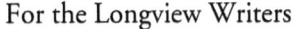

For the Longview Writers

Contents

Prologue

The Tao of Politics Anthology is a compilation of four books in one volume. Three of the books—*The Tao of George W. Bush*, *The Tao of Red States and Blue States*, and *The Tao of Politics*—were published previously. *The Tao of America* is published here for the first time. Each book has its own explanatory notes, so I refer you to those for more information about the books individually.

Collectively there is more than a little variety to be found, from the humor in *The Tao of George W. Bush*, to the analysis in *The Tao of Red States and Blue States*, the philosophy in *The Tao of Politics*, and finally the patriotism in *The Tao of America*. There is therefore ample opportunity for the reader to find something herein to which he can relate, either positively or negatively.

I write a daily online blog, The Tao of Politics, (http://taoofpolitics. blogspot.com.) In many ways this book serves as the theoretical underpinning of my blog. You don't have to read this book to understand the blog, but reading this book will certainly give you a lot to think about, and a lot to talk about as well.

The Tao of George W. Bush

Preface

This is not a book of quotations by George W. Bush. Rather, it is intended to illustrate and parody how the author imagines the President might react to or interpret the *Tao Te Ching* if he were to read it. This is therefore a work of the imagination. It is not just a book about George W. Bush, however. It is also an authentic, somewhat tongue-in-cheek reading of the *Tao Te Ching*. The reader would benefit (i.e. gain more understanding) by becoming better acquainted with the ideas of both George W. Bush and the *Tao Te Ching*.

During the course of writing this work I consulted the 1891 James Legge translation of the *Tao Te Ching*. It is a rather antiquated translation, and my work owes much of its style to it. The italicized passages in this book were taken directly from the *Tao Te Ching*, and from Mr. Legge's commentary. The numbering scheme corresponds to the numbered sections of the *Tao Te Ching*. The reader can refer to the original in order to better understand the context of the excerpts.

I tried not to be too disrespectful to George W. Bush or to the *Tao Te Ching*.

Introduction

President George W. Bush attended the Asia Pacific Economic Cooperation (APEC) summit in October of 2003. In preparation for that trip he wanted to try and understand the Oriental mind. He therefore took a copy of the *Tao Te Ching* on vacation with him in August. He thought reading that book would help. Well, a day turned into a week, and a week turned into a month. When his vacation was finally over, he had finished reading and making notes on the *Tao Te Ching*. These notes were collected by Secretary of State Powell, and they form the text of the book before you now, unedited and direct from the pencil of the President.

1

Where the Mystery is deepest is the gate of all that is subtle and wonderful.

How now
Mysterious Tao?
What's in a name?
Originator of heaven and earth
Or the Mother of all things?
Mother of all things sounds
Too much like Saddam Hussein talking.
We've looked for his butt
All over heaven and earth.
Him and Osama bin Laden.
I bet they changed their names
And are hiding in some hole somewhere.
Snakes sometimes hide in holes.
In Texas we kill snakes.
No mystery in that.

2

All know the beauty of the beautiful, and in doing so know what ugliness is.

Knowing sorrow and loss
We are given the ideas of joy and gain.
Knowing defeat and death
We are given the ideas of victory and life,
And more defeat and death,
But for the evildoers.
Not for us.

The ideas of existence
And non-existence
Give birth to each other:
Existence for us,
Non-existence for the terrorists.
For all infinite justice,
Let it be so.

The sage manages affairs
Without doing anything,
And conveys his instructions
Without the use of speech.
I am a sage.

3

The sage constantly tries to keep the people without knowledge and without desire.

We must keep the people at rest.
Restless people are not happy voters.
We must keep them happy.
Empty their minds,
Fill their bellies,
Weaken their wills,
Strengthen their bones,
Give them a tax cut.
Give them another tax cut.
After all, it's not my money.
I get a big tax cut too
In my blind trust.

Sages don't hire really smart people
To work for them.
They don't hire people who disagree with them.
Or they get rid of them if they do.

The sage tries to keep people
Without knowledge and desire.
Too much knowledge and desire
And the sage might be out of
A job in 2004.

4

The Tao is like the emptiness of a vessel.

> Some people want to talk
> About the emptiness of a vessel.
> I don't understand what they mean.
> I'd rather talk about something else.

5

Heaven and earth do not act from any wish to be benevolent; they deal with things as the dogs of grass are dealt with.

Sages don't do things to be nice.
They do things because they're sages,
And because they've got it all figured out.

And what's all this about
The dogs of grass?
I like dogs
And I like grass.
At least I used to in college.
Sages treat people like dogs.
It says so in the Tao.
I don't have a problem with that.
As I said, I like dogs,
And I treat them pretty darn good.

6

The valley spirit dies not, aye the same; the female mystery thus we do name.

I have women who work for me.
I don't understand any of them.
There's something mysterious
About a woman.
But they're good to have around
Sometimes.

7

Heaven is long-enduring and earth continues long because they do not live for themselves.

The world's oil
Will last forever,
Or at least until 2008 which,
Politically, is the same thing.

Unselfishness has
Its own rewards:
Those who donate
Large sums to my
Re-election campaign
Will benefit from
My next tax cut.

8

The excellence of a residence is in the suitability of the place.

The best house is in
The best place, like Crawford, Texas.
Not Washington, D. C.,
Where you can't even
See the stars at night.
It's important to see the stars.
It keeps your mind peaceful.
There is a great deal of
Virtue in that.

The best times are
Those spent in Crawford,
Like August, the whole month,
Working on the ranch
And then going on the road
To raise money.

9

When one's work is done, and one's name is distinguished, to withdraw into obscurity is the way of Heaven.

I'd like to withdraw
Into obscurity
And be like I was before;
But I have more taxes to cut,
More deficits to raise,
More wars to fight,
More elections to win,
And if I'm lucky
I get to appoint some justices
To the U. S. Supreme Court.
That's worth sticking around for,
Especially if I need their votes
In the next election.

10

In loving the people and ruling the state, cannot he proceed without any purpose of action?

In doing my job, I don't have to appear
As if I have any purpose of action at all.
It says so in the Tao.
I can also appear
To be without knowledge sometimes
If I want to,
And sometimes I want to.
You just don't understand
Such mysterious things,
But I do,
So get off my back.
I'm the one who's ruling the state,
Or the country,
Which is the same thing.

11

Clay is fashioned into vessels; but it is on their hollowness that their use depends.

> Empty space can be very useful.
> A pot is useful because it is empty.
> A door is useful when it is open.
> A room depends on the empty space within
> To be a room.
> Remember that
> The next time you're
> Criticizing me.

12

The sage seeks to satisfy the craving of the belly, and not the longing of the eyes.

It is OK to eat all you want.
In fact it is necessary
For a growing, healthy economy.
In the words of JFK,
Ask what you cannot eat
For your country.
Also, ask what you can eat
For your country.
You cannot eat French cheese
And French wine.
You can eat all things
American, in large quantities.
What better for the world's
Only superpower than
Everything and everyone
Supersized?

13

Favor and grace would seem equally to be feared.

Those who have lots of things
Could end up losing them.
This leads to worry and fear.
That is the way of the Tao.

If you don't have anything,
You can't lose anything,
And there is no cause
To worry.

For example, there is a bright side
To not having a job.
You can't lose something
That you don't have.

So those who are unemployed,
Or living in poverty,
Cheer up.
Things can't get any worse,
Unless you die,
And don't worry
We won't kill you.

14

We look at it, and we do not see it, and we call its name 'Equable.'

Many things cannot be
Seen or heard or
Held in your hand.
Like the deficit:
You can't see that;
But a tax cut,
You can hold that
In your hand.
You can spend it
To help your family
Or just to buy something.
I think people would rather
Concentrate on what they can
Hold in their hand
Instead of on what
May or may not
Be in the bush.

15

Who can make the muddy water clear? Let it be still and it will gradually become clear. The skillful masters of old comprehended the mysteries of the Tao.

Anyone can muddy the water.
Who can leave it alone
And let it become clear?
Anyone can stir up
Restlessness and impatience.
Who among us can wait?
My tax cuts will
Stimulate the economy
And improve the lives
Of our citizens.
Many wise men of old
Agree with me on this.
Listen to the wise men.
Quiet your mind.
In fact, don't think about
Anything at all.
It works for me.

16

All things go through their processes of activity, and then return to their original state.

Cycles.
Sometimes you're up,
Sometimes you're down.
They're all just cycles.
That's why I don't
Pay any attention
To polls.
It's where you end up
That counts.
In 2000 I ended up
On top.

The economy?
They're all cycles too.
Five year business cycles;
Stock market, bond market,
Housing starts.
There's only so much
You can do about
Any of that.
But I'm doing what I can
To stimulate the economy.
And it's where all that ends up
That really counts;
Whether, like my daddy,
I get credit for it
Or not.

17

In antiquity the people did not know their rulers.

> Sometimes the people
> Love their leaders.
> Sometimes they
> Fear them or despise them.
> I know a lot of people despise me,
> Some even in the Middle East,
> But they can't vote
> So what do I care?

18

When the Great Tao ceased to be observed, benevolence and righteousness came into vogue.

Benevolence and righteousness
Have not always been in vogue.
Sometimes there was hypocrisy.
Sometimes there was dissonance,
Like when the Dixie Chicks
Said those things about me.
They should be glad
I'm so benevolent.

19

If we could renounce our sageness and discard our wisdom, it would be better for the people.

> I can't renounce my sageness
> Or discard my wisdom.
> I wish I could.
> I can't renounce
> My benevolence
> Or discard my righteousness.
> I've got a job to do
> And I'm going to do it.
> Those who scheme for gain,
> As well as the hypocrites
> Should be ashamed of themselves.
> No, I'm talking about the Democrats.

20

When we renounce learning we have no troubles.

> My mind may be that of a stupid man.
> I may be in a state of chaos.
> Ordinary men may seem brilliant,
> While I may seem dull and confused.
> But who's the President of the United States?
> Come on and say it:
> George W. Bush.

21

The grandest forms of active force come from the Tao, their only source.

> The grandest forms of active force
> Come not from Tao, their only source,
> But from Army, Navy,
> Marines, Air Force;
> Brave men and women in the course
> Of daily duties every one,
> Fighting battles that must be won,
> To make the world a safer place
> For you, me, and the whole human race.
> Even the Arabs.

22

He whose desires are few, gets them; he whose desires are many goes astray.

My desires are few.
All I want is
87 billion dollars
For the war in Iraq,
Etc.

That could be a lesson
To you all:
Don't go astray.
Be humble and distinguished.
Be a sage like me.

23

A violent wind does not last for a whole morning; a sudden rain does not last for a whole day.

When it rains it pours.
An ill wind,
Well, something, something.
The fire of Heaven and Earth
Rains down upon the evildoers.
All's right with the world.
And if it's not,
I'll fix it.

24

He who stands on his tiptoes does not stand firm. He who displays himself does not shine. He who vaunts himself does not find his merit acknowledged.

Who stands on tiptoes anyway?
Women, some types of men,
Sometimes people changing light bulbs.
I want an order going out
To all the troops:
"No standing on tiptoes!"
Why, you might as well wear
Tutus and toe shoes.
No one respects someone on tiptoes.

Also, you can't display yourself,
At least not in public,
Or vaunt yourself.
I don't even know what that means
But it doesn't sound good.
Everybody understand?
Shape up or ship out.

25

Heaven is great. Earth is great.

> The American people are great.
> They elected me.
> Even though I didn't get
> The most actual votes,
> I got the ones that counted most.
>
> The people deserve
> A President like me.
> Why, I never could work
> Those punch card ballots either.
> So I understand
> Where you're coming from.
> And I understand
> Where you're going.
> Let's go there together.
> Wait a minute,
> Do I go two blocks this way
> And turn right?
> Or is it left?

26

Gravity is the root of lightness; stillness the ruler of movement.

What goes up must come down.
It's called gravity,
Like with the bombs
Falling over Iraq.
It's that way, I think,
With the stock market too.
It's not my fault
That so many people
Lost money in their 401k's.

I know I haven't said much lately
About investing social security
In the stock market.
That doesn't mean I think
It's a bad idea.
I've just been busy trying to prove that,
Unlike my father,
I can win a war
And still be re-elected President.

27

The skillful traveler leaves no traces of his wheels or footsteps.

The skillful President,
Like Teddy Roosevelt said,
Walks softly and
Carries a big stick.
I've got the biggest stick
Any President ever had,
And I'm not afraid to use it.
Just ask the people of
Afghanistan and Iraq.

The terrorists may have caught us
With our pants down,
But we've pulled them up
And buckled our belt.
They can't see our stick,
But they'd better watch out.
They're on our list,
And they know
Which list
I'm talking about.

28

He who knows how white attracts,
Yet always stays within black's shade,
In the unchanging excellence arrayed,
Return to man's first state has made.

I think I'd like to be called
"Your Excellecy."
Yeah, that has a good ring to it.
I like it when they play
"Hail to the Chief."
They could play that,
And then announce,
"His Excellency, George W. Bush."
Yeah, that sounds good.
Maybe I should do
A Presidential Proclamation.
Where are those Proclamation forms
Anyway?

29

If anyone should wish to get the kingdom for himself, I see that he will not succeed.

> The Tao says I'm going to win
> The next election.
> All those Democrats
> Who want my job
> "Will not succeed."
> Maybe after the election
> I'll get a throne
> For the TV room.
> I think I'd like
> To watch the Super Bowl
> While sitting on a throne,
> Eating a bag of pretzels.
> I also wouldn't mind
> Having a court jester.

30

A skillful commander strikes a decisive blow and stops. He does not dare to assert and complete his mastery.

I don't know how
These people ever won
Any wars way back then.
Some of their ideas
Are plainly stupid.
But who knows,
Maybe it's because
Of the weapons they had?
You can't do much with
Bows and arrows,
Swords or stones.
Give them a couple of
Cruise missiles,
A B1 bomber;
Keep the nuclear option
On the table
And they'd change their tune.
War may be contrary to
The spirit of the Tao,
But let me know
When the Tao
Finds Osama bin Laden.

31

Weapons, however beautiful, are instruments of evil omen, hateful.

> I know I'm not going to convert
> To Taoism any time soon.
> They're against war,
> And I've already won two of them.
> I might even wage a few more
> Before I leave office.
> And those Taoists
> Are probably against
> Capital punishment too.
> No, I'll stay with Christianity.
> That way I get to have
> More fun.

32

If a leader could hold onto the Tao, everyone would submit themselves to him.

Everyone submits themselves
To me as it is.
I've got the bombs, the planes
And the fighting men.
Who's going to stand in my way?
Oh, I know France
Does some grumbling
Every now and then,
But if push came to shove,
We'd be doing all
The pushing and shoving.
They'd throw a hunk of cheese
And we'd throw a hand grenade.
Who needs the Tao
When I've got a god-awful big
Military budget?

33

He who does not fail in the requirements of his position will continue long.

Now that's more like it.
I've done a good job.
I've won two wars
And given two tax cuts.
So again, according to the Tao,
I should be re-elected in 2004.
Sometimes I like what
The Tao has to say
And sometimes I don't.
I like this.

34

The influence of the Tao is felt in the vegetable world.

The Tao may be OK
In the vegetable world,
But in the world of
Bombs and missiles,
Terrorists, armies
And planes
You'd better let me
Be in charge.

Hold on!
I just remembered that
Monsanto has to be in charge
Of the vegetable world.
I guess that leaves the Tao out.

35

The benevolence of the Tao is inexhaustible.

> The benevolence of
> The American people
> Is inexhaustible.
> So are our abilities.
> In this way
> The Tao is a lot like we are.
> But the truth is,
> The Tao could learn
> Some things from us:
> Our resourcefulness,
> Our patience,
> Our resolve.
> How to make a
> Peanut butter and jelly sandwich.
> How to grill a hot dog.
> How to set off fireworks on holidays.
> Boy! The good old
> American Way.

36

Instruments for the profit of the state should not be shown to the people.

The Tao says that a leader
Can keep the people
In a state of simplicity
And ignorance.
It also says
I don't have to tell
Anybody everything about
What the government does
With its money.
I don't always agree
With the Tao,
But this is one time when
I do.

37

The exercise of government should be according to the Tao, doing without doing, governing without government.

I'm all for smaller, simpler government
And I don't think Washington
Has all the answers.
I think Washington needs
To get out of the lives of more people
Especially corporate CEOs,
Who are the backbone
Of our economy,
As are everyday
Hard working people.
No, Washington needs
To get after the terrorists.
Hunt them down,
Pin them down,
Neutralize them.
Ha, ha, I like that word:
Neutralize.

38

The great man dwells with the fruit and not with the flower.

Flowers are pretty,
But fruit is pretty too
If you think about it.
Besides, you can eat fruit.
It tastes good
And it's good for you
Although sometimes
It may be a little messy.
Who wants to eat flowers?
Maybe Flower Children,
Not me.

39

They do not wish to show themselves elegant-looking as jade, but prefer to be coarse-looking as an ordinary stone.

You may prefer
To be coarse-looking
As an ordinary stone.
I prefer to look like jade.
Wait a minute.
Jade is green, right?
OK, then, I'd rather be a ruby.
No, it's "better dead than red"
Isn't it?
What about a sapphire?
Blue? Maybe not.
Oh, I've got it:
I'd like to be a diamond.
Diamonds are
Somebody's best friend
Aren't they?
I need all the votes
I can get.

40

The movement of the Tao by contraries proceeds.

Republicans and Democrats
Are contrary to each other.
Sometimes it's hard
To get anything done.
When we do get things done,
Like a law passed,
Things like that,
It is not because
Of this contrariness.
It's because we have
More votes then they do.
So help me out in 2004.
Send more Republicans
To Congress.
I appreciate it.
(This message paid for by
Really rich people
Getting richer while
I'm in office.)

41

Scholars laugh greatly at the Tao. If not, it would not be worthy to be called the Tao.

> I'm glad I'm not
> The only one
> Who feels like
> Laughing at the Tao.

42

The Tao made One; One made Two; Two made Three; Three made All Things.

You know, I don't feel too bad
For not understanding
All this stuff.
Even the guy who
Translated it and
Wrote the commentary
Is just as baffled
As I am sometimes.
What's that they say
About the Oriental mind?
Inscrutable?
Yeah.

43

The softest thing in the world dashes against and overcomes the hardest.

> I would have thought
> That would be
> The other way around,
> With hard things
> Dashing against soft things.
> At least that's
> The way it works
> Where I come from.
> Get my drift?

44

Of life or wealth, which is more dear?

Sometimes the Tao
Sinks into absurdity.
No one wants to lose his life.
All the stock options
In the world are not
Worth losing your life.
Of course, there is such a thing
As martyrs.
Some people do want to die,
Like those hijacking evildoers,
Or Osama bin Laden.
Well, in some instances
I'd be happy to oblige them.
I sent a lot of men
To their deaths
When I was in Texas.
I'll be happy to do the same
In Washington, D. C.
Just ask Timothy McVeigh.

45

Do thou what's straight
Still crooked deem;
Thy greatest art still stupid seem,
And eloquence a stammering scream.

I never liked Shakespeare, you know.
All that playing around with words,
Acting cute, just seemed stupid to me,
Made me want to scream.
I couldn't even understand
What he was talking about half the time.

This passage seems like MS:
More of the same.
Well, I'm a man of plain talk
And few words.
No, wait a minute,
That's John McCain.
Well anyway, I don't like
All this flowery talk.
It's for flower children,
Not for me.

46

There is no guilt greater than to sanction ambition.

Some of this is getting to be
Like a broken record.
OK, so according to the Tao
You're not supposed
To want anything.
Well, just how far has that
Gotten the Chinese,
Huh?
More than a billion people
Poverty, problems at home;
And who's number one
In the world,
Huh?
We're number one!
We're number one!

47

Without going outside his door, one understands all that takes place under the sky.

This passage sounds like
They're talking about
The Weather Channel.
But they didn't have
TVs back then.
Do they have TVs now?
Probably, but I doubt that
The peasants have one.
They have a lot of
Peasants over there.
If China would ever get its
Act together, we could
Do some business with them.
We could sell them TVs,
Cable, satellite dishes.
Then they could check out
The Weather Channel
And find out what's
Really going on
Under the sky.

48

He who devotes himself to the Tao seeks from day to day to diminish his doing.

OK, first they say
You're supposed to
Want nothing.
Then they say
You're supposed to
Do nothing.
No wonder the Chinese economy
Is in the shape it is.
That's not the way it works
In this country.
We want a lot
And we'll do almost
Anything to get it,
Especially when it comes to
Things like oil.

49

To those who are not good to me, I am also good.

This reminds me
Of the Christian idea
Of turning the other cheek,
And that's all well and good,
But when the evildoers
Smite us on one cheek,
I think it is OK
For us to smite them back.
That's the only way
We can get them to stop
Doing evil.

50

The rhinoceros finds no place in him into which to thrust his horn.

> You say that a rhinoceros
> Can't hurt you?
> That's foolish.
> If a rhinoceros
> Comes running after you,
> You'd better take
> Evasive action
> Or kill him.
> I didn't say to run.
> In this country
> We never run.

51

All things without exception honor the Tao and exalt its outflowing operation.

> Now it sounds like
> They're talking about God,
> You know like in the hymn
> "Praise God from whom
> All blessings flow."
> If that's true,
> Then I can understand it
> A lot better.
> In any case,
> I'm sure the Tao
> Is on our side
> In the war against terror.

52

Who uses well his light,
Reverting to its source so bright,
Will from his body ward all blight,
And hides the unchanging from men's sight.

> Once again the translator
> And commentator admits that
> Even he doesn't understand
> One of these passages.
> Great. Now I don't feel so alone,
> Or dumb.
> Besides, maybe it's the Tao
> That's dumb.
> Did you ever think of that?

53

If I were suddenly to be put into a position to conduct a government according to the Great Tao, I should be most afraid of a boastful display.

> Should I be "most afraid
> Of a boastful display?"
> Well, I've often talked of humility,
> So I don't plan to be boastful.
> Should I "carry a sharp sword?"
> Well I'm going to.
> I don't care what the Tao says.
> I'm a compassionate guy,
> But that only goes so far.
> Compassion in the face of evil
> Is evil.
> I really believe that.

54

Tao when nursed within one's self,
His vigor will make true;
And where the family it rules,
What riches will accrue.

OK, first the Tao says
You're not supposed
To want anything.
Now is promises that
"riches will accrue"
If you let it rule your family.
Then it says you'll thrive
And have good fortune.
It doesn't sound to me
Much different than
The promises of some politicians,
"Pie in the sky," so to speak.
Well, I promised tax cuts
And you got tax cuts.
You got to hold them
In your hands.
You could have bought
A lot of pie with them.

55

Poisonous insects will not sting him; fierce beasts will not seize him; birds of prey will not strike him.

> If anyone thinks
> He's safe from
> Poisonous insects,
> Fierce beasts and
> Birds of prey
> Just because he follows the Tao,
> Then he's not as smart
> As he'd like you
> To think he is.
> Heck, that's like saying
> We're safe from terrorism
> Just because we follow the Tao.
> Well, given a choice between
> A gas mask and the Tao,
> I'll take the mask.

The infant's virile member may be excited, showing the perfection of its physical essence.

> I don't know about China,
> But in Texas we don't
> Talk about the "virile member"
> Of little boy infants.

56

He who knows the Tao does not care to speak about it; he who speaks about it does not know it.

Trying to understand the Tao
Is like trying to find
Osama bin Laden.
Whoever talks about him
Doesn't know him,
And whoever knows him
Doesn't talk about him.
But that's OK.
We'll hunt those outlaws down.
We'll bring 'em to justice.
That is the American
Way.

57

The multiplication of prohibitive enactments increases the poverty of the people.

> Well, you see?
> Poverty is not my fault.
> It is the fault of Congress
> For making all those
> Laws and regulations.

A sage has said, "I will do nothing and the people will become rich."

> So the Tao says that
> If I have a hands off policy
> Toward the people
> Then they will prosper.
> Well, if things get worse
> With the economy,
> Don't blame me,
> Blame the Tao.

58

The government that seems the most unwise, oft good things to the people supplies; too much meddling, touching everything, will often disappointments bring.

I can go along with this.
We've got to get government
Out of the lives of
The American people.
The people know how
To spend their own money
Better than the government does.
If all this seems unwise,
I don't care.
Take it up with the Tao.

59

There is nothing like moderation.

> I agree,
> There is nothing like moderation,
> But moderation is sometimes good,
> Sometimes bad.
> Good when faced with
> Things like fiscal spending;
> Bad when chasing
> The evildoers.

60

Governing a country is like cooking a fish.

> That's right:
> First catch it,
> Cut the head off,
> Gut it, scale it,
> Rinse it; then
> Fry it, broil it
> Or grill it.
> The point is,
> It's a lot of work,
> And we use a lot
> Of energy.
> It doesn't matter
> Which kind of
> Energy we use,
> But if we don't tap into
> Those oil reserves up in Alaska,
> Some of the fish won't get cooked.
>
> Also, as with #59,
> Cooking a fish is another case
> When you don't want moderation.

61

The great state must learn to abase itself.

Just when I think
The Tao is making sense,
It goes and throws
A passage like this one at us,
Telling us we must learn
To abase ourselves.
Well, America is a great state,
And we're not going to
Abase ourselves before anyone.
No, we're standing tall,
Talking softly,
And don't forget about
That big stick
I spoke of earlier.

62

Why was it the ancients prized this Tao so much; the reason why all under heaven considered it the most valuable thing?

You know, East is East
And West is West,
And they'll forever
Remain far apart.
In the East, in China
They worship the Tao
As their salvation.
Out West, in Texas,
We worship God
And Jesus.
Out West, we think
Jesus is the most valuable
Thing under heaven,
And take it from me,
That's not going to change.

63

It is the way of the Tao to conduct affairs without feeling the trouble of them.

This is what happened
With us in Iraq.
We saw a tyrant who
Needed to be toppled,
So we went in
And toppled him,
Never thinking about
The trouble involved.
Heck, trouble's
Our middle name,
Or one of our names, anyway.
We'll never shy away
From trouble,
'Cause if you don't
Face trouble in
The light of day,
You'll have to face it
In the dark of night.
I like to sleep at night.

64

That which is brittle is easily broken. That which is small is easily dispersed.

Al Qaeda is not small anymore.
At one time it may have been easy
To break them, but that was before
I became President.
I've done a good job
Of dispersing them though.
They couldn't cluster around under
All those bombs we dropped
In Afghanistan.
So they've been dispersed,
And they're pretty brittle now too.
But we've got to keep it up,
And take the fight to them
If we're going to break them for good
And get me re-elected next time.

65

The difficulty in governing the people arises from their having too much knowledge.

I've often thought this was true.
So I've never really wanted
To tell the people very much.
Sometimes when you don't, though,
They end up finding out anyway,
Like when they discovered how
We edited that EPA report.
Nothing much happened,
Of course; it was just a bunch
Of bad publicity for awhile.
I don't care about bad publicity.
I think the people will vote for me
No matter what the press says about me,
Especially as long as I say
We're still at war.

66

The sea is able to receive tribute from all the valley streams because it is lower than they.

There is a big difference
Between the Tao and me.
The Tao relies greatly on
Water images and abasement.
I rely on muscle.
With enough muscle
You can make the water flow
Wherever you want to,
Like with the Panama Canal.
I still hate that we
Had to give that up.

67

I have three precious things which I prize and hold fast: gentleness, economy and shrinking from taking precedence of others

I have three precious things too:
Truth, Justice and the American Way.

Three more things:
The code of the West,
Having a good dog,
And going to church regular.

I could go on with many more,
But you get the idea.

68

He who fights with most good will, to rage makes no resort.

Good will?
I've got nothing against
The Iraqi people.
I've got nothing against
Arabs at all,
Except for those who
Blew up our Twin Towers,
Took a big chunk
Out of the Pentagon,
And who continue to plot
Against us.
Those were acts of war.
All I've got to say is
Don't start something
You can't finish,
'Cause we'll finish it for you.
Otherwise, I'm pursuing
The war on terrorism calmly,
Without rage, and with the utmost of
Good will,
Even for the French.

69

There is no calamity greater than lightly engaging in war.

> Excuse me, I beg to differ.
> It would be a greater calamity
> If you were against
> The United States,
> Either as an enemy,
> Someone helping the enemy,
> Or just as some
> Misguided nitwit
> Who's always got to pick
> The wrong side of every cause,
> Like those Taliban guys
> We captured in Afghanistan.
> We all know where they are now,
> Don't we?
> Gitmo.

70

My words are easy to know and easy to practice; but there is no one in the world who is able to know and able to practice them.

>I can't figure out
>What the heck
>To say about
>This passage.

71

To know and yet to think we do not know is the highest attainment; not to know and yet to think we do know is a disease.

Once again I'm speechless.

72

When people do not fear what they ought to fear, that which is their great dread will come to them.

I think that's what
Happened on 9/11.
We weren't prepared,
And so we got hit.
I'm not sure I would use
The word "fear" so much.
We weren't "alert"
To what we ought to fear.
Well we're alert now.
And we're on alert,
Sometimes orange,
Sometimes red.
I don't like yellow alert.
We're not yellow.
Never were,
Never will be.
I think we need to find another color
For that.

73

It is the way of Heaven not to strive, and yet to skillfully overcome.

That may be OK for Heaven,
But in the real world,
Today's world,
That attitude
Will get you left behind;
If not worse, dead.
Striving is at the
Cornerstone of everything
We hold dear.
You can bet your boots
That other people and
Other countries are
Out there striving.
That's one thing that
Makes America great:
We're better strivers than
Anyone in the world.
Let's keep up the good work!
Go, USA!

74

The people do not fear death. Why try to frighten them? If people always feared death, who would dare to do wrong?

This seems to be an argument
Against capital punishment.
Believe me, I've heard them all.
Well, you've got to be tough
With criminals
Because they're tough.
When I was governor of Texas,
I sent a lot of guilty people
To the Great Hereafter.
They may not have feared
Death in Texas,
But they feared me
Because I was no nonsense.
Don't believe me?
Just try me.

75

The people suffer from famine because of the multitude of taxes consumed by their superiors.

> Well, I hate to say
> I told you so,
> But I told you so.
> Let's have another tax cut.

76

What is firm and strong is below, and what is soft and weak is above.

Here we go with the
Weak sister stuff again.
Well, there are no
Weak sisters around here,
And no room for any either.
Just ask Pfc. Jessica Lynch,
A hero in every respect
And in no way weak.
Go ahead, ask her.

77

May not the Way (or Tao) of Heaven be compared to the bending of a bow?

Oh, so "Tao" means "Way."
Interesting,
As in the Frank Sinatra song,
"I Did It My Tao."
Or the Burt Bacharach song,
"Do You Know The Tao To San Jose?"
Or the expression, "No tao, Jose!"

I don't like it.
It doesn't sound right.
They should change
The name of this thing,
Make it so Americans
Can understand it.

78

There is nothing more soft and weak than water; yet for attacking things, nothing can take precedence of it.

Water again!
What is this,
Chinatown the movie?
I drink a lot of water,
Take plenty of showers,
Wash the dogs,
Water the lawn.
Someone else does the dishes
And the windows.
If I want to blow up
A military target,
I'll use a Stealth Bomber
Not a garden hose.

79

When a reconciliation is effected between two parties after a great animosity, there is sure to be a grudge remaining.

> I don't have anything
> Against the French
> After our animosity.
> The French Mind is like
> The Chinese Mind:
> You can't figure it out sometimes.
> So I don't hold a grudge.
> Heck, I never liked them
> Much to begin with.
> That hasn't changed.

80

I would make the people return to the use of knotted cords instead of the written characters.

I hope they don't still
Have this attitude in China.
It's kind of hard to sell
TVs, Cell phones and
Automobiles to people who
Are still living in
The nineteenth century
B. C.!

I want a better life
For everyone.
One hand washes the other,
To use a little water imagery here.
You buy our stuff,
We all benefit.

81

Sincere words are not fine; fine words are not sincere.

Whew!
I'm glad I'm done with
This *Tao Te Ching*
Thing!
I agreed with some of it
And some of it I didn't.
I just wish they'd
Fix the spelling and
Pronunciation of their words,
As fine and sincere
As they may be.
After all, it's not
Hao nao braon cao;
And it's not
The Tow Jones Industrial Average.
Come on guys,
Get with the plan.
You know English is
The world's language
Or should be.

Conclusion

Reading the *Tao Te Ching* and making comments on its verses was challenging and tedious for the President at best, touch and go at worst. He was only able to persevere with a steady diet of peanut butter sandwiches and milk, not to mention various forays onto the campaign trail to raise money for his re-election. When his vacation was over and he had finished reading the *Tao Te Ching*, with a little help, no doubt, from Dr. Rice and others, he had less respect for the Oriental mind than he had to begin with, and he felt better justified in going out and telling the Pacific Rim countries what to do.

The Tao of Red States and
Blue States

Everyone who watched TV or read the news during the last two Presidential elections has heard of Red States and Blue States. Basically the Red States were the ones won by George W. Bush, and the Blue States were those won by his opponents—Al Gore in 2000 and John Kerry in 2004.

Thinking about Red States and Blue States reminded me of Chinese Philosophy. As the reader may know, yin/yang is a concept that deals with opposites such as dark/light, female/male, night/day, etc. The Red States and Blue States have qualities that are antithetical to each other too. In this book we will examine some of those qualities, particularly as they relate to the teachings of the *Tao Te Ching*, a 2000 year-old Chinese manuscript of wisdom and advice.

The Tao of Red States and Blue States is not intended to be a scholarly work. It is more a work of art. It is also an opinion piece of sorts. In writing this book I relied on the knowledge and beliefs I acquired while following the news for the past several years. I also relied on my imagination and on a detailed reading of the *Tao Te Ching.*

The Tao of Red States and Blue States is not a theory of Politics. It is a theory of, or philosophy of a media image, of dynamics between the two major political parties, and of election results, all from a Taoist perspective. The focus, therefore, is quite specific.

I hope this book will stimulate the reader to think and to do research for himself. He may find it interesting to read the *Tao Te Ching* in conjunction with reading this text. Each passage in this book is essentially based on a passage in the *Tao Te Ching.* I have therefore numbered my passages to correspond with their numbered counterparts in the *Tao Te Ching.* The reader also may find it interesting to read the *Tao Te Ching* independently. I consulted the 1891 James Legge translation while writing this book, but there are many other translations available that are more modern and readable. Those of Stephen Mitchell and Ursula K. Le Guin come readily to mind.

Finally, I tried to be impartial while writing this book. I hope I succeeded.

There is nothing about its name that makes a state Red or Blue. There is nothing about its location or its climate or its pace of life. There is something about the hearts and minds of men and women, an appealing candidate with an agreeable message, whether the message appeals to the heart or to the mind or to both, or to something else unknown. All that and more makes a state Red or Blue. (1)

Knowing a Red State, we can easily imagine a Blue State. Knowing someone from a Red State, we can easily imagine someone from a Blue State. They don't value the same things we value. They don't believe the same things we believe. By and large, however, you can't tell a Red State person from a Blue State person just by looking at him or her. There is something inside, not outside, that makes a person Red or Blue.

Given the idea of Texas, we can easily imagine more Red States. Given the idea of Massachusetts, we can easily imagine more Blue States. The only problem is that often we deal in stereotypes in which everyone who votes Red lives in a certain area of the country, and everyone who votes Blue lives in a certain area of the country. But that's just not true. Some Blue voters live in Texas and some Red voters live in Massachusetts. (2)

In the exercise of Politics, the Reds seek to not excite the Blues, and the Blues seek to not excite the Reds. The more excited each side is, the more likely they are to vote. Neither side wants the other side to go out and vote. (3)

The idea of Red States and Blue States is a recent idea. As a concept, however, it is not new. Political divisions have always existed, just as yin and yang have always existed. In both cases, the concepts awaited the particular graphical representations that we see today: in the former case, a map of the United States with some States colored Red and some colored Blue; in the latter case, the familiar yin/yang symbol from Oriental art. Red States and Blue States are not as absolute, black and white, as are yin and yang, but they are just as evenly divided. (4)

Red States and Blue States
Could be compared to
The two sides of a bellows,
To two men arguing,
To two lovers loving,
Or to any number
Of pairs of opposites.
When one side
Interacts with the other side
Something is produced
Or destroyed.
That is the Way of the *Tao*.
Indeed, that is the Way of the world.
We don't always like what results from
This interaction of opposites.
That is particularly true
In politics.
But at least in
The Red States and Blue States
We must accept the results. (5)

Red States and Blue States could be compared to a father and a mother: when a man and a woman come together and make a child, one never knows beforehand what offspring will result. And though we are not always surprised by who is elected when the Red States and Blue States vote, we are usually surprised by the manner in which he is elected. (6)

The Red States and Blue States may continue for a long time, or not.

In some instances it is easier for a Blue State to become a Red State than vice versa.

Some States will always be Red. Some States will always be Blue. Some States may change from election to election. They are called Swing States. (7)

The *Tao Te Ching* says, "The excellence of a residence is in the suitability of the place." Red States are suitable in some ways, and Blue States are suitable in other ways. Red States are more suitable at certain times of the year, and Blue States are more suitable at other times of the year. Some States are more suitable for certain activities than other States. And each State has its own unique offerings of food. But in some instances, what one person finds suitable another person finds unsuitable. (8)

The Blue States say that Government can help solve many of our social problems.

The Red States say that Government is part of the problem.

Meanwhile the rich get richer and the poor get poorer. (9)

In ruling a State, there seems to be a choice between helping disadvantaged people or helping large corporations. And it seems that the Reds make the latter choice, whereas the Blues make the former. (10)

You can't have a Red State without Blue voters. It wouldn't make sense. A State is Red not because there were only Red votes, but because there were more Red votes than Blue votes. That's what Red means. Take away all the Blue voters and you might still have a Red State, in some sense, but not the same Red State. (11)

When we look at a Red State we see blue sky and green everywhere, but no red, except perhaps in the red of a flower, the sky at sunset, the colors of certain sports teams, etc. But the same is true of a Blue State: same red sky/blue sky that we find in a Red State. So it's not the sky that makes a State Red or Blue. It is an election. (14)

When we look at a State, we may ask ourselves, "Where is the Redness that makes that State Red? Where is the Blueness that makes that State Blue?"

As hard as we look, we will never see those qualities with our eyes, for they are in the hearts and minds of the people who live there and vote. (14)

It is not enough for a candidate to craft a message that appeals to his constituency of Red or Blue. He must craft a message that motivates his constituency to actually vote. A State can become Red, for example, by an absence of Blue voters, as well as by an abundance of Red voters. Turnout is key.

And some may say, isn't a candidate who "crafts his message" being phony and not genuine? These days, with focus groups and pinpoint polling, a candidate must craft his message. Either that or lose. (15)

People vote for candidates they like and trust, and with whom they can identify. We have all seen men lose elections because they seemed out of touch with regular people. If you want to win a Red State, then Red State voters must like you, and you must appear to like them, perhaps to the point of being one of them.

It's not the same with Blue States. Just look at Al Gore and John Kerry. With all the baggage that those two had, the Blue States voted for them anyway, and they came within a hair of winning it all. So the Blue States are looking for something different in a candidate than are the Red States. It therefore seems that if you had a Blue candidate who somehow appealed to Red voters, he would automatically win all the Blue States, some of the Red States (one or two might be enough) and thereby the election. Does John Edwards fit this scenario? Wesley Clark? Mark Warner?(15)

The time between Presidential elections is a time of relative stillness, at least on the surface. In reality there is a great deal of activity. Some of the activity begins when the last election ends. Much of it begins at least several years before the next election. During that in between time, a State that was Red still has the potential to become Blue, and a State that was Blue has the potential to become Red. Some States have a higher probability of making that change than do others. (16)

Some voters are swayed by lies while some voters are not.
Some campaigns contain more lies than others.
Some campaigns are about nothing but lies.
Some States have become Red or Blue because of lies.
Some States have become Red or Blue in spite of lies. (17)

There don't seem to be many checks or balances on voters, unless you count not letting children or convicted felons vote, etc. Voters are free to be just as dumb or just as intelligent as they want to be. Voters are free to believe what they want to believe, or decide however they want to decide. Why, they're even free not to vote. When all is said and done, and all the votes are counted, they count them Red or Blue. But the votes of these individuals don't count as much as the votes of the States in the Electoral College. That's where an accumulation of Red States or Blue States determine the election of one candidate or another. Except in 2000 when there were five Red votes and four Blue votes in the U. S. Supreme Court. In that case those were the votes that counted the most. (18)

In this country we have always had Red States and Blue States. That is the nature of the political process. It is a winner-take-all system, where whoever receives the most popular votes in a State wins all that State's electoral votes. It is only recently that the graphical representation of Red and Blue on a map of all the States has come to be used. If it had been used fifty years ago, the Solid South would have been Blue. Today the South is still solid, but it's Red. (19)

Blue States have just as many dumb voters as Red States do. Red States have just as many informed voters as Blue States do. It's just that when Red State voters and Blue State voters think about their choices for President they somehow reach different conclusions and vote accordingly. (20)

Is there something we can identify and say, "This is the essence of a Red State or a Blue State?" In some ways you'd want to say that a Red State is Republican and Conservative, whereas a Blue State is Democratic and Liberal. But these qualities are not absolute. Red States have voted Blue, and Blue States have voted Red, at least historically speaking. Of course there are exceptions. The District of Columbia, it seems, has always voted Democratic or Liberal, and therefore could be essentially Blue. Kansas could be considered essentially Red, as could most of the Great Plains States, despite the fact they voted for Lyndon Johnson in 1964. The Northeastern States are essentially Blue, despite the fact they voted for Nixon and Reagan during their landslide years. But what is the essence of Redness or Blueness? We're still looking. (21)

The sage manifests humility to all the world. In recent years we have heard our politicians speak about humility, but have we seen them manifest it? George W. Bush has been in power now for awhile. Before that it was Clinton of the Blues, Reagan/Bush Red and Carter Blue. You might have to go all the way back to Ford, if even then, to find a humble President, and he wasn't elected to the office. The Presidency is not about humility, although it could be. I don't think a humble man could be elected President. A candidate might say he was humble, like George W. Bush did in 2000, but was he truly humble or was that just rhetoric? It takes a great deal of pride and even some arrogance to run for President, much less to win. In Presidential Politics humble guys finish last. (22)

Do the Red States and Blue States agree on anything? Of course they do. It is difficult to notice any agreement, however, especially during an election year because they are so busy disagreeing with each other. During a non-election year it is the representatives of the Red States and Blue States in Congress who perpetuate the contentious atmosphere.

What are some things that everyone agrees with, or should agree with? They can be found in the Declaration of Independence and the Constitution. (23)

The candidates stood up, with ideas clearly distinguishable from each other, and political parties came forth, Republican and Democratic. From these parties came the ideas of Red and Blue, in the minds of the media, in the minds of the voters, and in the minds of thinkers, political and non-political, trying to make sense of this dichotomy. Where did it come from? Where is it going? Where could it go? How could it be changed? What does it mean for me? What does it mean for the country? So far, there are so many questions, known and unknown, and so few answers. (25)

What goes up will come down, eventually, and in what could be called something like "The Political Law of Gravity," what is Red today could be Blue tomorrow. A politician can never take anything for granted. If he does he runs the risk of becoming an ex-politician. (26)

The men and women behind a President, advising him, telling him what to do, often leave no trace of their advising and telling, but their influence is often just as important as that of the President himself. Their advice can get us into a war or keep us out, for example; and in political campaigns, it is they, by their strategic decisions, who often decide which States become Red or Blue. (27)

Relations between Red States and Blue States can be compared to relations between men and women. In an election, one type of State, Red or Blue, is clearly dominant, whereas the other type of State, the losers, like it or not, must submit to that dominance. Relations between men and women are often struggles for dominance as well. (28)

The Presidency is within anyone's grasp. All you have to do is figure out how to put together the most electoral votes from the Red States or the Blue States. Of course a candidate must choose a color, Red or Blue. He can't be both Red and Blue.

If a candidate wins a State, it becomes his color. A State is not any color really until people vote and the votes are counted. But after the votes are counted, and when the results become clear, the State is designated a particular color, and it remains that color for the next four years. (29)

Making a State turn Red or Blue requires decisive action. Any hesitation, any passivity can cost valuable votes. A candidate and his advisors must be firmly rooted in political reality, which is not necessarily the same as actual reality. (30)

In the political climate of the early twenty-first century it seems that the Red States are more militant than the Blue States. Of course everyone can support a war if it is necessary, but not everyone can support a war if it seems merely expedient, and this is one reason the Blue States now differ with the Red States: some of our recent military action has seemed to be unnecessary, not to mention expensive. (31)

The relationship of Red States and Blue States to the electoral process is like the relationship of the ocean to all the great rivers and streams which feed into it. And whoever best controls the electoral process, in great measure determines the distribution of Red States and Blue States. (32)

Red States and Blue States
Help us make sense of
And validate
An often chaotic
Capricious
Complicated
Controversial
Election process. (32)

Voters who think
The country is moving
In the wrong direction
Will not always vote for change.
If they did,
There would have been more
Blue States in 2004
Than actually voted that way. (33)

The Red States are always trying to achieve a permanent majority over the Blue States, and vice versa. This is true with regard to the Presidency and both houses of Congress, as well as the Governors' mansions, and State legislatures throughout the country. Such a permanent majority seems unlikely, but if it did happen it would permanently define the character of the United States as perceived by those at home and abroad. It is doubtful whether or not that is a good thing. (34)

Red States and Blue States both seek to be the center of attraction for voters, but in the final analysis one always succeeds better than the other.

And then there is the matter of benevolence: are the winners always benevolent to the losers? Are the losers always benevolent to the winners? The struggle that ends on election night often begins a conflict that continues until the next election. (35)

The Red States and Blue States are not passive entities. They are active in electing a President. The height of their importance occurs on the day when the Electoral College meets to cast and count their votes. After that, they stand as an emblem of the election just held, a symbol which serves to legitimatize the man who was elected President. (37)

Red States and Blue States
Do not always vote
For a candidate
Who is entirely truthful.
Often they vote
For a candidate
Who says what they want to hear.

Some States abide by what is solid.
Some States abide by what is soft.
Some dwell with the fruit.
Some dwell with the flower.
But the choices they make
Have a profound and lasting
Impact on our nation
As a whole,
Not to mention
The whole world. (38)

A man is never satisfied with a majority of votes from the Red States or Blue States. If he has a winning margin, he wants a mandate. If he has a mandate, he wants a landslide. Presidential candidates have egos much larger than the proportion of votes they receive. (38)

When we look at the different parts of a Red State, we do not see what makes those parts add up to become a Red State. The sky is just as blue in a Blue State as it is in a Red State. The grass is just as green in a Red State as it is in a Blue State. But Red States depend on Blue States for their existence. If there were no Blue States, there would be no need for Red States. The color scheme was invented to indicate differences, not similarities. Yet wherever you look, similarities are all you see. It's too bad the people living there often can't find more common ground for agreement. (39)

It has been said there's not a dime's worth of difference between the two major political parties, the Republican and the Democrats, the Red and the Blues. But that's not true. There is more than a dime's worth of difference. In fact, in many ways, the Reds are really opposite from the Blues.

The Republican mind is different from the Democratic mind. It is not genetic, or anything like that, but Republicans just believe different things, and think in different ways than Democrats do. This becomes obvious when you listen to the two sides debate a topic of social importance; also when you listen to pundits from opposing sides give their spins on things. (That is, if you can listen to the spin without becoming ill.) There may not be a dime's worth of difference between politicians and spinmeisters, of whatever ilk, but positions taken by opposing parties on important issues often could not be more distinct from each other. (40)

The United States
Is United
In spite of,
Or perhaps because of
Red States
And Blue States. (41)

One nation produces one election.
One election produces two, Red and Blue.
Red and Blue produce
One winner
One President
One nation
Which adds up to
One. (42)

The battle for supremacy in Red States and Blue States is not for the meek or the soft. It is for bold and tenacious fighters. The boldest and most tenacious stands the best chance of winning in a contest where winning is everything, and where the outcome will have an impact on the course of history. Therefore one should not minimize the process which results in a State's becoming Red or Blue. (43)

Red or Blue?
Which is the most precious
For our nation and her people—
All her people?
This is a question
That is rarely,
If ever answered
On election night. (44)

Reds act on things that Blues regard as unnecessary.
Blues act on things that Reds regard as unnecessary.
In the exercise of our Government,
Depending on which side is in power,
And to what degree that power exists,
Someone always gets to complain
That their needs and wants
Are not being met. (45)

Thomas Jefferson said we have a right to the Pursuit of Happiness.
But some people are happy when the Reds are in power,
And some are happy when the Blues are in power.
Under our political system it seems that
You can't make all the people happy all the time. (46)

It is easier to vote in some States than in others.
It is easier to get it right in some States than in others.
It is easier to count all the votes in some States than in others.
It is easier to make you vote count in some States than in others. (47)

The more information some people have, the more inclined they are to vote for a particular candidate. The more information other people have, or think they have, the more inclined they are to vote against a candidate. Politicians know this about voters. That is why they sometimes run negative campaigns. If they can't get you to vote for their man, maybe they can get you to vote against his opponent. So the distribution of Red States and Blue States often reflects something negative rather than something positive. (48)

A man does not run for President by himself,
And he is as good or as bad
As those who are helping him.
A bad candidate can be helped to win,
And a good candidate can be helped to lose.
In the end it all depends
On how his message is received
In the Red States and Blue States. (49)

It is sometimes more important for a candidate to display a winning attitude than for him to talk about the issues. This is one of the paradoxes of Politics. A State can sometimes be influenced to vote Red or Blue by factors having nothing to do with logic or truth, right or wrong. (50)

Red States and Blue States don't really exist until everyone has voted and the votes have been counted. The States are then assigned a color based upon the outcome of the vote.

It would not be incorrect to say that the concepts of Red States and Blue States mean nothing and they mean a lot. Before the polls close on election day, color is potential only. After the polls close, and until the next election, the colors have their meaning, of which everyone has his own understanding and interpretation. (51)

When you're in a Red State you might think you know what kind of people you'll meet, just as when you're in a Blue State you have a preconception of what kind of people live there. And some of the stereotypes are correct. There are lots of rowdy rednecks and brusque New Yorkers, for example. But the main thing you find, if travel from State to State, Red or Blue, is that the people who live there are not that much different from me and you. (52)

The word *Tao* means "Way." This is an important concept in Politics. For example, there is a Red State Way, with all that encompasses, and a Blue State Way, equally complex. We could ponder these concepts for a long time and probably never fully explain them. And their meaning changes according to who the candidate is. The Red Way of George W. Bush is different from that of George H. W. Bush. The Blue Way of John Kerry is different from that of Al Gore. The flexibility that each Way possesses is one of its greatest sources of power. (53)

If our country were a garden
Planted here with
Red flowers,
There with Blue,
Then every four years
The flowers are dug up
And the garden
Is planted anew.
They are watered
And nourished
By a long campaign.
Then on election night
And on succeeding days
The flowers come out
In full bloom. (54)

People who were born in Red States rarely move to Blue States. But many people who were born in Blue States seem to be migrating to Red States in droves. Ask most any Southerner, for example, and he can attest to the fact that things are noticeably different "since all those Yankees came down here." Needless to say they're not overjoyed about all that. But the Northerners are not always that happy either. They sometimes don't fit into their new surroundings and have trouble feeling really at home, spiritually or politically. But if enough people from Blue States move to Red States, that might turn a Red State into a Blue State. The transplanted Northerners might be happier then. (55)

There is something noble about a President, but there are many things about Presidential candidates that are not noble. In order to win a Red State or a Blue State, a person must engage in Politics, and Politics can be really unsavory. If the path to the White House was all about serving the Red States and Blue States then it might be different. A Presidential campaign might be nobler. But it is also about power, and as we know power corrupts, hence the lack of nobility often displayed in running for President. (56)

Can a Red President be elected from a Blue State, or a Blue President be elected from a Red State? I'm sure both Rudolf Giuliani (R) of New York and John Edwards (D) of North Carolina have thought about these questions as the 2008 election approaches. Of course any candidate can be elected from anywhere. Ronald Reagan came from California, which has recently been a solid Blue State, and Bill Clinton came from Arkansas, which is essentially a Red State. But since the last eleven elections have been won by candidates from the Southern half of the country, geography may be an important factor in determining our next President. Maybe Giuliani and Edwards will think about that as well. (57)

In some Blue States there is a Red State hiding just beneath the surface, waiting to be brought out. Given a few different votes here or there, the result itself would be different. The same is true of Red States, just not as many of them. The Red States seem to be more firmly Red, whereas some of the Blue States seem to be more up for grabs. For example, I can't imagine Kansas going Blue, but I can imagine California going Red. In fact, California was Red in every election from 1968 through 1988. A State, therefore, is usually one color or the other only in retrospect, not looking forward. (58)

In order to know what kind of plant you have, it is sufficient to examine its seeds or roots. Oak trees grow from acorns. The roots of a daffodil don't resemble those of a rose.

In order to know what color a State will be, one can examine its political roots. They are sometimes just as unambiguous as are those of a flower. But sometimes they're not, and that's why we have the election. (59)

Winning the Red States and Blue States
Is like eating a small fish:
You want to eat all the meat
And leave the bones for your opponent. (60)

In putting together
A majority of votes
From Red States or Blue States
Sometimes a small State
Is just as important as
A large State.
Ask Al Gore, 2000. (61)

A Blue State is not bad because it votes for the loser in an election, and a Red State is not good because it votes for the winner. Voting is one of our fundamental rights. Simply exercising that right is good, and in some ways not exercising it is not good, although everyone is free to vote for anyone they choose, or not to vote at all. At the end, when all the votes are tallied, and the results are known, the losers may say the outcome was bad and the winners may say it was good, but history will have the final say. (62)

An electoral majority begins with a small core of Red States or Blue States, then grows as more people make up their minds, decide to vote or not to vote, whatever. Many factors go into determining the outcome of an election, even the weather. But thank God that when it rains, it falls on Republicans and Democrats equally. (63)

The election of
A President
Begins with a single vote.
The election map
Of Red and Blue
Begins with a single State. (64)

Do Red State people
Dislike Blue State candidates?
Do Blue State people
Distrust Red State candidates? (65)

When the Red States dominate, the Blue States have the blues.
When the Blue States prevail, the Red States see red.
It is difficult to have a happy nation
When half its citizens are disgruntled. (66)

Between the Red States and Blue States
There are three precious things:
Cooperation
Compromise
Consensus.

Too often we find
Conflict
Contrariety
Contention. (67)

A Presidential campaign is like a war, and the electoral map of Red and Blue is like a map of the battlefield, of territory won and lost. Even some martial terminology is used, as when we talk about battleground states, etc. But a campaign is not a war. No shots are fired; no lives are lost. The whole process is entirely peaceful, as one might expect from a nation of laws. And no blood is shed, only tears of joy and disappointment. (68)

Much of the *Tao Te Ching* uses ideas that seem strange to Americans. For example, "I do not dare advance an inch; I prefer to retreat a foot." How many people would agree with that? Not many, I'm sure, and certainly not many American politicians. (69)

Sometimes it seems
That a State
Is more easily swayed
Red or Blue
By a lie
Than by what's true. (70)

No one,
From any State,
Red or Blue,
Has a monopoly
On what's false
And what's true. (71)

Do more
Thinking, caring,
Inquiring voters
Live in Red States
Or in Blue States? (72)

A Presidential candidate
Is like a fisherman
Who casts his nets
Into the sea
And hauls in States—
Large or small,
Populous or not,
Red or Blue—
Then hoists them
Onto the scales
To weigh his catch
Against the other side.

The winner has his photo snapped,
Posing with his prize.
The loser gets to grouse
About the one that got away. (73)

Everyone is more fearful now than they were before 9/11. Fear can influence elections, sometimes tipping a State from one color to another. Politicians know this, and they play on these fears. Sometimes the outcome of an election hinges on which candidate gets out the clearest message of fear. (74)

Many questions dealing with taxes tend to separate Red State voters from Blue State voters. It would be nice if these issues could bring people together instead of driving them apart. (75)

We've all heard the philosophical conundrum: If a tree falls in the forest, with no one around to hear it, does it make a sound?

If the people have spoken, but no one was listening, did they say anything?

If a person votes Blue, and his State becomes Red, does his Blue vote count? How? Where?

If 51 million people vote Blue, and 50 million people vote Red, what does it mean if Red wins? (76)

We hear much discussion in the news of surpluses and deficits, and it's good that we do, but in many instances they are just talking about numbers. The surpluses and deficits that are the most important are the ones that are the most difficult to quantify. It would be nice if we had a surplus in Washington of honesty, altruism, virtue, amity, justice, and respect for the law. Outside Washington it would be nice if we had a surplus of good will between the Red States and the Blue States. (77)

The Blues were in control of the White House for eight years during the 1990s. Did they look for ways to include the Reds in the national dialogue?

The Reds are in control of the White House now. Are the Blues being included or excluded?

Does either side really care about what the other side thinks? Or are they so focused on building majorities and pursuing agendas that consensus is ignored? Majorities may come and go, but consensus has a way of healing. (78)

The Red States and Blue States should seek to reconcile with each other as soon after an election as possible. But this sort of harmony is not always sought and rarely achieved.

It would be better for our leaders to hold fast to the needs of our nation as a whole than to focus too much on the needs of the Red States or the Blue States. (79)

The graphical representation of Red States and Blue States illustrates (but often exaggerates) the size of a Red State majority, which in terms of actual votes cast may be quite small, or even nonexistent, but in terms of geographical area looks quite large. (80)

What is the Way of
Victory? Is it
The Red State Way
Or the Blue State Way?
This is a question
That must be answered
Every four years. (81)

Here are two websites that the reader might find interesting and edifying:

http://answers.google.com/answers/threadview?id=415905

http://en.wikipedia.org/wiki/Red_state_vs._blue_state_divide

There may be other references via Google or other search engines. One good thing about the Internet and other research tools is that you never know what you'll find until you start looking.

The Tao of Politics

The Tao of Politics was conceived while I was writing *The Tao of Red States and Blue States*. I realized then that I wanted to do a closer examination of political theory, but not at all from a traditionally Western point of view. There is enough of that out there on the airwaves and in the Blogosphere. Politics in this country and in this century seems so polarized, much like the yin/yang of Chinese Philosophy, that I decided there must be more moderate ways to approach it. It never hurts to look at subjects from different, non-traditional points of view. When we do we often arrive at different understandings, different conclusions. That is what *The Tao of Politics* seeks to accomplish.

I hope this book will stimulate the reader to think and to do research for himself. He may find it interesting to read the *Tao Te Ching*, a 2000 year-old Chinese manuscript of wisdom and advice, in conjunction with reading this text. Each passage in this book is essentially based on a passage in the *Tao Te Ching*. I have therefore numbered my passages to correspond with their numbered counterparts in the *Tao Te Ching*. The reader also may find it interesting to read the *Tao Te Ching* independently. I consulted the 1891 James Legge translation while writing this book, but there are many other translations available that are more modern and readable. Those of Stephen Mitchell and Ursula K. Le Guin come readily to mind.

Which came first, Politics or Government?

There is Politics and then there is Politics.

Politics is governing, and Politics is seeking to govern.

Politics by any other name is still Politics. (1)

We may not like Politics.
We may not like
The way it is conducted.
But the flip side
Of the coin
Is Anarchy.

Besides,
We can change
The way Politics
Is conducted.
That's one good thing
About Politics. (2)

In the exercise of Government,
Truth is of the utmost importance.
But not so
In the exercise of Politics.

These days almost any politician
Would say almost anything to get elected
Or re-elected.
And it often works.

It would be good
If the people were
As responsive to the truth
As they are to deception
And lies.

But then
They'd have to
Think critically,
Wouldn't they?
Do the people
Think critically?
Could they do it more? (3)

A politician's words are
Among his greatest assets.
When he speaks,
Everything about his being
Is focused on persuasion:
His face, his voice,
His body language
All come together
In one grand message
Received by the listener.
A great politician
Is a great communicator
Who somehow connects
With the electorate. (5)

What role do women have in Politics? They serve widely in both political and governmental positions. They can sit in a Governor's mansion but not in the White House. They serve as Presidential advisors but not as Presidents. Is this trend changing? Perhaps, but I don't think a woman is getting any closer to holding the highest office in the land. Politics is all about power. Men have it and women don't. That, among other reasons, is why you don't see a woman presiding in the Oval Office.

What about Hillary Clinton? As of 2005 we still have years to wait before we find out if she will ever be President. Don't hold your breath. (6)

When a President is re-elected,
And six months later
The people decide
He's doing a bad job,
Or they don't like his priorities,
What were they thinking
When they voted for him?
Probably nothing has changed
Since the election.
Don't blame those
Who voted against him. (7)

A political advantage continues
For a long time
Or for a short time,
Depending on how much
A politician is in tune
With the people who could elect him.

The successful politician
Appears to be doing a good job
While perpetually running for re-election. (7)

Those who reside in the White House
Are the most excellent, in some ways,
But not necessarily the most qualified.

The interesting thing about
The highest office in the land
Is that it goes to a politician—
And usually the best politician.
It doesn't go to a statesman,
A professor, or a CEO.
Think about that.
Most jobs have a list of
Qualifications an applicant
Must satisfy
Such as education,
Work experience, etc.
Not that of President.
If there are no qualifications,
Then one might say
The job could just as easily go
To a charlatan or a con man.
Maybe sometimes it does. (8)

The excellence of a mind is in seeing a problem clearly, thinking about it dispassionately, and solving it honestly.

The excellence of those in public service lies in the degree of their virtue.

The excellence of a public official is in his leaving Government better than he found it.

Excellence and mediocrity are relative. A candidate can be excellent in some aspects and mediocre in other aspects.

Everyone recognizes a man with an excellent intellect, but not everyone will vote for him.

Excellence in winning elections is not the same as excellence in governing. The best President is excellent in both. (8)

It is better to not be President than to be a bad President.

It is better to think about the job at hand than to think about a legacy.

Can we ever say enough about humility? (9)

A President had better know what he is doing.
He has the fate of the free world
And of future generations in his hands.
That is an awesome responsibility. (9)

Politicians want to rule the State
But do they love the people?
All the people?
The greatest leaders do.
What do politicians love?
Money? Power?
The answer to this question
Serves as a measure of their greatness
Because it reflects how they lead.

What a politician
Says he loves
And what he
Actually loves
May be two different things. (10)

A politician's effectiveness
Depends on the people he represents.
His power comes from
His constituency.
The most effective politicians
Remember that.
The least effective
Don't.

The people
Have more power
Than they realize. (11)

Sometimes we see a politician
Satisfy the cravings of his belly,
While many of his constituents go hungry.
He may satisfy the longing of his eyes,
While his constituents go wanting.
He may be successful as a public servant,
But he's not a true servant of the public. (12)

Some politicians must feel invincible,
Or maybe they are simply arrogant.
Otherwise they would not engage in activities
That sometimes bring them such disgrace.

One good thing about being President:
Those who suffer disgrace
Or those who do a bad job while in office
Usually have a chance to redeem themselves
Once they leave office.

Some disgraces
Are worse than others,
Though they may not
Be recognized as such. (13)

The National Debt
Must seem to voters
Like an abstraction.
And politicians
Must know this
As a fact.
Otherwise everyone wouldn't
Cooperate so much
In letting it grow
And get so out of hand. (14)

What a politician says
And what he means
Are not always
The same thing.

There is directness
And there is spin.
These two are not
At all the same thing.

Politicians say one thing
And then do something else,
Yet we still keep
Electing politicians. (14)

The Master Politician knows how to
Turn a discussion to his own purpose;
How to say something without really saying it;
And how to answer questions
Without really answering them.
The Master Politician is a magician
With ideas, arguments, and words. (15)

Who can make
A clear discussion obscure?
A politician.
Who can make
An obscure discussion clear?
A great politician.

No one can sling mud
And not get dirty
Like a politician. (15)

There are two major political parties in the United States.
They don't always agree with each other.
They are not always kind or magnanimous to each other.
It is difficult to have good feelings
Throughout the entire nation
When one political party
Is intolerant of the ideas of the other party.

There is never a time when Politics ceases.
Political activity is more evident at certain times than at others.
Some Politics we see happening, some we don't.
If we don't see any Politics happening,
Cable networks will find some to show us. (16)

Some people fear some Presidents.
They fear what they will do:
Start a war,
Increase poverty,
End abortion,
Damage Social Security, etc.
Sometimes these fears are not borne out.
Sometimes they are.
For those who fear a particular President,
The night he is elected is bad.
All their fears seem to be suddenly realized.
It either gets better or worse after that. (17)

Some of the people
Will always hate
Some of our leaders,
No matter who
Our leaders are, or how
Benevolent they are.

Some people hated Lincoln.
Some hated Roosevelt.
Some still do.
In Politics, hate is on
An equal level
With love. (17)

Disharmony between the political parties
Leads to disorder in Congress.

What is hypocrisy?
Saying one thing
And doing something else?
How many of
Our politicians
Are hypocrites? (18)

In our political system, the people get to "speak", at least for President, every four years. After the election the winner can say, "The people have spoken." Does that mean we have to be silent in between elections? No. In fact every citizen has a duty to speak out and offer his opinion about matters of national and local importance. And every politician has a duty to listen, even in non-election years. (19)

What will a President focus on,
The desires of special interests
Or the needs of the people?
His choice will determine
If he is a great President
Or not. (19)

We need Presidents
Who have great intelligence
And judgment.

We need Presidents
Who really use War
As a last resort,
Not as something else.

We need Presidents
Who value
What the people value. (20)

The people have a right
To know the truth.

Sometimes it seems
That the sole purpose of Politics
Is to obscure
And conceal that truth. (21)

He who desires little
From the Government
Becomes a Republican.
He who desires a lot
Becomes a Democrat. (22)

Three things are
Characteristic
Of politicians,
In contrast to
The humble sage
Mentioned in the *Tao*:

Self-assertion
Self-boasting
Self-complacency.
All this stems from
Lack of humility.

Does anyone know
A humble politician? (22)

Asking a politician
To abstain from speech
Is like asking
A river
To stop flowing. (23)

A politician
Owes his existence
To Heaven and to Earth.
Why then honor one
And not the other? (23)

Politics should be
Less about self
And more about
Selflessness. (24)

Heaven and Earth
Are great,
But there is
No Politics
In Heaven. (25)

A politician who is indifferent
To the plight of the people
May be a good politician
But is he a good man?
Politics needs
More good men. (26)

Politics
Above all things
Is a social art.
He who would succeed
In Politics
Must be a master
Of social skills. (27)

Everyone needs
Balance in their lives,
Even politicians.

No one wants
A weak politician.

The world has a way
Of corrupting people,
And maybe more so
With politicians. (28)

Public office is for those
Who go out and grasp it.

The nature
Of Politics
Is such that
What is up today
May be down
Tomorrow,
And vice versa. (29)

When a
Politician becomes
Commander-in-Chief of
Our nation's armed forces,
Sometimes he sends
Our soldiers to die for
Political reasons. (31)

The relationship of Politics to Government
Is like that of sex to a large family:
While some may consider the former to be dirty,
Yet we must engage in it in order
To ensure the existence of the latter.

For some, Politics is just as enjoyable as sex.
For some, Politics leads to sex.
For some, sex leads to Politics. (32)

A President,
Either alone or
With the help of Congress,
Can undo much that
His predecessors have done.

A President should take his agenda
From the people,
Not vice versa.

A good leader knows how to follow.

The people are wiser than the President.

Most Presidents are devious to some degree. (33)

Wherever you find
Men and women
And property
You'll find Politics.
You can't get away
From Politics.
It's like language:
It's everywhere,
With everyone.

Of course,
The best way
To get away from
Political language
Is to turn off your TV. (34)

Many are attracted by it,
And many are repelled, but
Everyone respects the power
The Master Politician wields.

With that respect
There is often
A measure of fear. (35)

In a political campaign, a candidate's words are the major thing we have on which to base a decision about how to vote, but often we are wrong to believe those words. (Remember, "Read my lips! No new taxes!"?) So what are we to do? We can't get rid of the politicians. We need them.

Maybe all we can do is just trust the system, as imperfect as it is, and hope that someone really unscrupulous doesn't lie his way into office and do any permanent damage. That seems like a strange position to be in. Shouldn't there be more accountability for politicians, for what they say and what they do? (36)

"Governing without
Government" sounds like
Political rhetoric:
An interesting thought,
In which many
Could believe,
But impractical
And impossible
To achieve. (37)

It is difficult
To completely trust
The system when
The system seems to
Sometimes make mistakes,
And we are left to
Wonder, "Isn't there
A better way
To do some things?"

Of course we have no choice.
We must trust the system.
Maybe it can't be
All things to all people,
But shouldn't it try? (37)

A great man
Is often great
In spite of the fact
That he's a
Politician.

Politicians speak of "values."
Sometimes that is
Political rhetoric.

Do politicians
Value anything
As much as they value
Money and votes? (38)

It would be nice
If we had more
Clear-cut choices
For President.
Sometimes we're voting,
At least in effect,
Not for our first choice
But for the lesser
Of two evils.

Like it or not,
When a person votes
For a politician
He implicitly votes
For his entire agenda,
Known and unknown.

Sometimes a politician
Can transcend the pettiness
Of Politics. (39)

Politics works somewhat like the *Tao* works:
Opposing forces are pitted against each other
And one side prevails. But the main thing
About Politics: it's not all black and white. (40)

Those who don't think
Politics can be
A laughing matter
Must not watch
Leno, Letterman,
Olbermann,
Et al. (41)

Men dislike
Favoritism
Inequality
And injustice
Until they become
Politicians. (42)

Politicians
Could learn something
From the Doctors:
First do no harm. (43)

Don't let Politics
Get in the way of
Politics. (44)

What would Politics be
Without personal ambition?
Good Government. (46)

A politician
Believes whatever
The voters believe. (49)

A politician can improve his own life
Or he can improve the lives of the voters.

A politician can defend the people
Or he can leave them defenseless.

A politician can send men to die
Or he can work for peace.

A politician can be responsible
Or he can be irresponsible. (50)

Politics is the source of all Government, good and bad.

Politics produces much that the people need
And much that they don't need.

The nature of Politics is such that,
Though there is good and bad,
The system works for the benefit of all,
But not as well as it could. (51)

Politicians and the people
Complete each other.

Politicians should honor the people,
Not vice versa. (51)

Politicians are great when
They call upon
The best qualities of men
And not the worst.

No matter how
Politicians
Might juggle it,
The Truth remains
Unchanged. (52)

For a politician to pamper himself with eating and drinking, and with a super-
abundance of property and wealth, while many of his constituents go hungry or
go without, is surely not the way Politics was intended to be conducted. (53)

In Politics,
Whatever is detrimental
To the well-being of a nation
Will eventually end
If the voters are
Unselfish, aware,
And determined enough
To end it. (55)

A politician can increase
Prosperity or poverty,
Order or disorder,
Either by what he does
Or what he doesn't do,
How he rules
Or how he doesn't rule.
That is an awesome
Responsibility. (57)

Government is supposed to exist by the consent of the governed. One question is, do we all consent to what our government is and does right now? We should think about that. If we don't consent, we need to do something. If we don't do something, then that is a tacit consent. (58)

Government is big,
That's a fact.
The question arises,
Will Government
Be good for the people
Or not?

There is a big difference between
A Government's meddling in people's affairs and
A Government's helping people who need help.

Politics? Government is found by its side.
Government? Politics is found by its side.
Who knows how to separate the two? (58)

Everyone has limits
On their behavior.
Some politicians
Don't know their limits
Or they forget them.
When they exceed their limits
They get into trouble
Just like everyone else.

There is nothing quiet or small
About the rise or the fall
Of a politician. (59)

Governing a State
Is like cooking a fish:
The smaller the fish
The more people
Who go hungry.

To some it seems
That the top two percent
Of the people
Eat all the meat
And leave the bones
For everyone else. (60)

If all men are
Created equal,
Then why aren't they
Always treated equally?

To say that all men are created equal
Without acting to back that up
Is to pay lip service to an ideal
Nothing more.

Politicians could ensure
The equality of men.
So far they haven't. (61)

Politics is a
Valuable thing.
It has such a huge
Potential for good,
And yet sometimes it
Is underutilized
Or utilized for ends
That are not always good. (62)

Some politicians would have us believe that
In conducting the affairs of State
The most important things to accomplish
Are sometimes the most unpopular
And often the most difficult.

Sometimes they are right about that,
But sometimes they are wrong. (63)

Some of our grandest ideas,
Those upon which
Our Government was founded,
May have begun in the mind
Of one person. (64)

Politicians thrive
When the people are
Simple and ignorant
And believe everything
The politicians say.

Intelligent,
Informed people
May keep
Politicians
Honest. (65)

Politicians must form a good relationship with the people.
Loners don't get elected to anything.
In a political contest, the politician with the
Closest relationship to the most people
Will probably win. (66)

There are many precious things
Which we hold dear.
Most of them, like Truth and Justice,
Are abstract concepts
Which are seemingly easy to ignore.

Sometimes it seems that
Politicians either don't value
The same things we value,
Or they value their own versions of them. (67)

The best politician contends
With his opponent honorably
And still wins.
He bends men's wills to his own,
And in the end
He unites the nation behind him. (68)

There is no room for passivity in Politics, and yet we see it a lot. For example, in the Presidential campaigns of Mike Dukakis and John Kerry, they both failed to respond to attacks at critical times, and they both lost.

Rule #1 for political campaigns: No Passivity! (69)

It is easier to judge a politician
By his actions than by his words,
Except in a political campaign,
When his actions and his words
Both might be tailored to win votes.

Much about Politics is also about deception. (70)

We rely on our leaders
To keep us informed.
Sometimes they keep us
Misinformed. (71)

Sometimes in the heat of a Presidential campaign the voters fear what they have no reason to fear and hate what they have no reason to hate. They often base their votes on these irrational feelings. After the election, when reality sets in, it is too late to take their votes back. (72)

Politicians may think they are above the law,
Or that they have their own morality,
But it is rare that someone,
Even a very powerful man,
Escapes with impunity
The consequences of his actions. (73)

If a politician can't stir up
Positive emotions about himself,
He will often try to stir up
Negative emotions about his opponent.
In fact, the latter is often easier,
More prevalent,
And more effective. (74)

People were concerned about taxes even two thousand years ago, so I guess not much has changed. That seems paradoxical. The *Tao* is supposed to be all about change.

Many politicians disagree about taxes. Many citizens do as well. We can all agree that some Government is necessary. The Founding Fathers seemed to think so. And you can't have Government without taxes. So it just becomes a question of how much of each do we want or need? (75)

The people aren't
Difficult to govern,
At least not by
A Government which is
Just and benevolent. (75)

You can't get elected President
Without friends.
But once you are President
Your friends should be the ones
Who voted for you,
Not just the ones
Who paid the bills
To get you elected. (79)

The politician
Doesn't have to make
Everyone happy,
Just the people who
Are likely to vote,
And likely to vote
For him. (80)

Some politicians try to improve their own lot.

Some politicians try to improve the lot
Of a small group of people.

Some politicians try to improve the lot
Of all the people. (81)

The politician
Tries to master
At least the appearance of
Sincerity.
The better he masters that,
The better politician he is. (81)

This book is not the last word on the subject of Politics. There is a lot more that could have been written, and a lot more waiting to be written. With that in mind I have started a new political blog, The Tao of Politics (www.taoofpolitics. blogspot.com) where we will continue to seek alternative ways of looking at and talking about issues of current interest. Join us there when you get tired of politics or media coverage as usual.

The Tao of America

Much has been written about America. I did not consult any of those other works while writing *The Tao of America*. Instead, I relied, for my inspiration, on the 1891 James Legge translation of the *Tao Te Ching*. That shouldn't seem too odd. If one is going to write "The Tao" of anything, he should consult Lao Tzu's book, which I did. Consequently I owe most of my debt to him, to my imagination, and to my many years of being an American.

The reader may find it strange to use a book of Eastern philosophy to help in discussing something as quintessentially Western as America. The *Tao Te Ching* is more universal than one might realize. What it lacks in universality can be made up for by interpreting some passages more broadly, and by ignoring certain passages altogether.

When I began, I wanted to think and write about America, land that I love. I could have used any number of models to guide me. I chose to use the *Tao Te Ching* because I wanted to explore the subject in a different way than had ever been explored before. As a result, I think I have something different here: a rather unconventional book about America. I hope it stimulates people to think about, and reflect on, what it means to be an American. I don't want people to take sides politically as a result of reading this book. *The Tao of America* is not Red or Blue. It is Red, White, and Blue.

NB: When you are finished reading this book, or really anytime that the spirit moves you, join me online at The Tao of Politics (http://taoofpolitics.blogspot.com) where we take a somewhat more partisan approach to the discussion of issues important to America.

You can call her the United States of America, the USA, America the Beautiful, whatever. But whatever you call her, the name only says a small part. America is much more than a name. She is a place on God's green earth, and an ideal that lives in the hearts of all those who call themselves Americans, or who dream of being called American.

America strives to be the source of all good in the world. In her efforts to do good, often she succeeds, and sometimes she fails.

America is not the only source of good in the world. The more she acknowledges that, the better the world will be.

Most of what is wonderful about America is not subtle, although her subtleties can be wonderful too.

America may seem to be a mystery when you're outside looking in. From the inside she is no mystery at all.

If we think of America, we might be reminded of all that is not America, the good and the bad, and we might feel impelled to take that opportunity to give thanks that we are Americans.

Everyone makes mistakes. We might feel the desire to learn from our mistakes, and to continually strive, as our forefathers said, to form a more perfect Union.

There was a time when America as a country did not exist, and the world was poorer for that.

America has always existed in the hearts of those who dream of freedom and of a better life for themselves and for their children.

Nothing is perfect except the ideal of America; and we, as Americans, are constantly striving to realize that ideal.

America thrives on competition. A large portion of her history is told by the stories of men who have competed and, more often than not, won. Some of them are mythical, like John Henry. Some of them are real, like Charles Lindbergh. But they are all heroes, our heroes. They are Americans, and they are larger than life, larger even than this land.

America always acts from a wish to be benevolent. America wishes no harm to any country or to any person. America cannot be pushed around, though. If she is, her wrath is swift and final. It may take her awhile, but she always wins.

Americans working together can accomplish much; but Americans working alone can also accomplish much. America is a nation of individuals. She celebrates and exalts the individual perhaps like no other nation on earth does. But America is like no other nation on earth.

When you have valleys, you also have hills.
When you have females, you also have males.

There is heaven, and there is earth.
There is America, and there is everywhere else.

America has not endured as long as many other countries have; but America was built on the ideals of freedom and justice. Those ideals have always existed, and will endure for all time.

Freedom and Justice are seldom perfect. Americans may not like this, but they understand it, because they know that the alternatives are much worse by far.

Americans are not shrinking violets. They do not withdraw from the world, or from life. Wherever there is a job to be done, they are often first in line to do it. They work in groups, and they work alone. Above all she is a nation of individuals, and as the individual goes, so goes America.

Americans don't love the backseat. They love the front seat, and they love to drive. That's why they have built so many highways. That's why they buy so many cars. And that's why they love oil so much.

Americans are always on the go: back and forth to work; back and forth to the mall; sitting in the drive-thru, waiting for some food. Americans love to eat in the car, while sitting at a stop light, or driving down the road. There is nothing that an American likes any more than having some french fries in one hand, and the steering wheel in the other.

No one ever accused Americans of being placid or contented. By European standards we may be considered to be rowdy, restless, and brash. We're certainly not staid or dull, and we're certainly glad of that. Some cultures may look down their noses at us, but we've been known to thumb our noses at them.

Has God ever made a land more beautiful than America? If He has, I would like to see it.

But her beauty is only one aspect of her greatness. Her true greatness lies in the ideas upon which she was founded, and it resides in the hearts of her people.

The people came here from far and wide, each one bringing something different to the pot, making a stew like no other in the world. And our greatest strength—diversity—could have been our greatest weakness. It has at times, in fact, been tested, but has always bounced back, even stronger than before.

Beauty? Nothing is more beautiful than watching and listening as a stand full of Americans cover their hearts and sing the National Anthem at a baseball game on a crisp October night.

America would not be the same if she were somewhere else. She has a particular blend of oceans, rivers, and lakes; mountains, beaches, and plains. Wherever you go in America, you see her natural beauty, of course, and Americans there to appreciate it.

People from all times and all lands have come to our shores, and left their old lives behind them to start a new life in America. For them, and for many others who never got to realize their dream, their highest aspiration was American citizenship. For those who achieved it, it was hard work; but the rewards were worth it. Forever after, their children and grandchildren, born in this country, were US citizens. And that seems to be a characteristic of American life: we become Americans so that our descendants will be Americans. We work hard, and often deny ourselves luxuries so that our descendants will have an easier life.

Americans definitely see the glass as half full, not half empty.

Americans take on tough jobs, like building a canal to connect two oceans, or flying to the moon and back. When we see a challenge, we don't back away. We persevere to the end. No one is as determined, resourceful, or indefatigable as we are. Americans succeed where others fail.

Americans do what no one else does.
Americans go where no one else goes.
Americans dream what no one else dreams.

The stories of many great American cities are told in the stories of her rivers, lakes, and ports. In this day of trains, planes, and automobiles, boat travel is just as important as it ever was. America would cease to function as it does without her rivers, lakes, and ports.

Americans are not really big on museums. Don't get me wrong, we have them. We have a lot of them. But we're not as big on honoring and preserving the glory of the past as we are on making new things today and looking to the future.

If someone were to come to America from outer space, he or she might think that our malls were museums, or houses of worship, or something important like that, mainly because of their enormous edifices, and vast parking lots, obviously designed to accommodate large numbers of cars and people at one time. In some ways that visitor from outer space might be right.

A lot of people might think that Americans are arrogant, and maybe we are. But that's all right. A lot of people from other cultures (like England or France) are arrogant too. The difference is that Americans often have good reason to be that way.

Americans love to work, mainly because we love to get paid, and we love to go out and buy things. When the work is done we take a break, have a beer; maybe throw a party, enjoy ourselves, and then look for more work to do.

Don't expect many Americans to withdraw into obscurity. America is not a nation of hermits.

If there is a mysterious quality about America, perhaps it is the fierce patriotism of her citizens. Perhaps that is a result of reciting the Pledge of Allegiance so much, or singing the National Anthem. Perhaps it is because of our fierce love of freedom and justice, our intense hatred of tyranny and injustice.

We have it pretty good in this country, and we'll fight to the last man if anyone tries to take that away.

There is a certain innocence and naïveté among some generations of Americans. We haven't had the devastating wars on our soil that have been seen by so many in Europe and Asia. We haven't had much of the suffering and privation experienced in the Third World. Some of that is beginning to change. The events of 9/11 brought the war home to us. Hurricane Katrina revealed the Third World right in our midst. And yet, for many, these tragedies are ephemeral, tied as it were to the news cycle: one bad story is pushed from our consciousness as another bad story takes its place. So far this cycle has continued unabated: tsunami, Natalee Holloway, London, Egypt, Bali, Karl Rove, Iraq dead, hurricane, hurricane, gas shortage, rising energy prices, pandemic just below the horizon—an incessant drumbeat of bad news, brought to us 24/7 by MSNBC, Fox News, and CNN. But the thing is, many of us can turn off the TV, walk outside, and still enjoy the silence of America. That won't change.

America is a vast country with vast resources, both material and nonmaterial. It may be a cliché to say that our most important resources are our people, but it's true. Many other countries have vast resources. How do they compare with us? There is no comparison.

As long as Americans remain true to America, the real America, and all that entails, our country will continue to lead the world.

If America didn't invent the neon sign, she certainly has put it to good use. And it serves, in a way, as the primary symbol of our culture. Whereas other countries, other world cities, may be older and more sedate, America is shiny, new, and exciting. Other cultures may seem to be rooted in history, while our culture seems to be rooted in the present, always pushing impatiently to the future, with neon signs often pointing the way.

America certainly is big on appealing to the sense of taste. We have whole industries devoted just to manufacturing flavors to put in the food. And it seems like the cheaper the food, the more flavors it has in it, mostly artificial of course, though you can't tell that by tasting it. They take something that has no taste to begin with, add a bunch of flavors to it, and make it so cheap that anyone can afford to buy it. Now that's Democracy!

America has known low points in her history: December 7, 1941; September 11, 2001; August—September 2005. We have good reason not to be complacent, although we have at times been lulled into a false sense of security, feeling safe and invulnerable. In recent months and years, it has seemed that our threats have come as much or more from nature as they have from men. How can we prepare for every disaster? We can't. But we can prepare our hearts and minds. It is during a disaster that a people find out what they are made of. Americans are courageous, generous, and resilient. We do not fear the low points because we know they only make us stronger as a nation.

The motto of the Boy Scouts of America is "Be prepared." The motto of the US Coast Guard is *Semper paratus*, "Always Prepared." These two American institutions help us know how to live and what to do as a people. Theirs is not a message of fear, but of maturity and responsibility. Let us look to all of our institutions for guidance on how to conduct our lives as individuals and as a nation.

America certainly has known her share of highs. Everyone has his or her own personal favorite: VE Day, VJ Day, the 1980 US Olympic Hockey Team.

Americans are winners. We don't have much experience losing, so our highs definitely outnumber and overshadow our lows. Will that ever change? Not as long as we maintain our indomitable spirit in the face of those forces, without and within, that would weaken us. And we will maintain that spirit. We are winners.

Truth, justice and equality cannot be seen, but these constitute the fabric that holds our nation together as one.

Similarly, lies, injustice, and inequality cannot be seen, but these are the things that can tear a nation apart.

Some would say that we have gotten away from the original America, the one created by our Founding Fathers, but does an adult ever really lose the child he once was? No, we're the same America, just a little older, and hopefully a little wiser, but maybe not. Many today disagree about the direction our country should take. Such disagreements can be constructive or destructive. Recently they have tended more toward the latter.

Everything changes. Our Founding Fathers were wise enough to give us a system that adapts well to change. Their system is still working. Today's America is the result. Our forefathers were wise enough to create America. We, today, must be wise enough not only to help her continue and flourish, but also to perpetuate the ideas, like truth, justice, equality, and liberty, that made her great.

All great nations seem to go through a rise and a fall, a climb to the summit, followed by a period of decline; all nations except America. The world has never before seen another nation like America, and it never will again. There is only one America, invincible, first among nations. When they write books about the future, it is America about which they write.

America is the world's only superpower. What does that mean? We are the only remaining country that can have a significant impact on a global scale—for good or for ill. Being a superpower carries with it a responsibility as big as the whole world, and as serious as life and death.

America has been lucky enough to have good leaders for the most part, leaders who have maintained our country's position of preeminence, or who have led us even higher. But perhaps luck has little to do with it. Perhaps the goodness of the American people has enabled us to choose leaders as good as we are. Let us hope it continues that way. America's future depends, in great measure, upon the goodness both of its people and of its leaders.

America is a benevolent country, but she is also capable of displaying her wrath. Historically she has been slow to take up arms, but once she did, she didn't put them down again until her foes were vanquished. And usually she has been on the right side of history. But whatever side she has been on, it has always been better for others if they were on America's side.

America attracts the best and the brightest from all parts of the world, and from all fields of endeavor. Everyone wants to come to America—to live, to work, to play, to get paid. For all these things and more, America is the best place on earth. No other country comes in a close second.

Americans are not people who are satisfied and listless, as if they had just eaten a huge meal (although they do often eat huge meals.) They are energetic, busy, eagerly pursuing their goals, doing their business; working hard, playing hard, always on the go; vibrant, alive, optimistic, and happy. This is the way a people are when they are building the future. These are Americans.

America, perhaps more than any other country in the world, is the source of the good life. Certainly it is possible for other people in other lands to lead good lives, and many actually do prefer their own ways of life, at least until they come to America. But Americans prefer America, and American ways. There is an ease about life in America that is found nowhere else on earth, for no other place is as good as America.

Americans are spoiled. In our own land, we are comfortable with the American way of doing everything. When we travel abroad, we immediately notice when things are not the same. Often we don't like what we find. Americans hold the world up to American standards. The world seldom measures up.

All things, it seems, are transitory, temporary; all things, that is, except America. Long live America, and prosper. The world depends on you.

Americans believe they can do anything, and often they can.

Heaven is great;
Earth is great;
America is great
And her promise is great
Because her people are great.

America has left her mark upon the earth, in many places, and in many times. People may argue about whether or not that mark has been always good, but no one can argue about the essential goodness of America.

Americans have left their footprints on the moon. No person from any other country can say that, and they probably never will.

There is right and there is wrong in this world. America is always on the right side.

When we count up and decide what has been the greatest force for good in the world, America will be number one, as she is in most things.

America is strong where other nations are weak, and excellent where they are mediocre.

Humility does not produce excellence.

When the philosophers spoke about the best of all possible worlds, they could have been speaking of America.

Some people are jealous of America—for her liberty, her prosperity, her many blessings—and they'd like to bring us down to their level. We'd like to bring them up to ours.

America's history
Has much glory
To be told.
America's future
Has much glory
Yet to hold.

America has many strengths. Her spirituality is one. Of course she also has her feet firmly planted in the real world, because that is where her people live their lives. But spirituality helps to make those lives better, and it makes America better as well.

War is contrary to the spirit of the Tao,
And it is contrary to the spirit of Heaven,
And it is contrary to the spirit of America.

Unfortunately war is not contrary
To the spirit of everyone,
And it is not contrary to the spirit of
Every country around the world.
That's why we fight so many wars.

The years may pass, but America will never grow old. After all, how could freedom ever grow old? And how could a creative spirit ever grow old? America is always making new things, remaking herself, and she will never grow old. She will live forever young.

There is nothing that America values more than she values peace.

Though some things about America are constantly changing, some things always stay the same, like the principles upon which she was founded, the goodness of her people, and the confidence that things will only get better as time goes by.

All rivers flow to the sea, and their waters accumulate there. America is like the sea. Americans have come from all over the world to this one blessed place, following this one beacon of freedom. Countries that are not free do not welcome people in with open arms like America does, nor do people yearn to go to countries that are not free. No other country offers the kinds of opportunities to so many of her citizens as America does. The opportunities are not always within easy reach of everyone, but we are always working to correct that.

American ideals existed before America came to be. Those ideals will always exist.

There will always be an America.

If there is a God, He surely must have smiled favorably on this land, because it does seem blessed.

Many things about America
Are inexhaustible:
Her energy,
Her optimism,
Her beauty,
Her benevolence,
Her spirit
To name but a few.

America hopes for a better life for all Americans, as well as for all mankind, and she is willing to work toward achieving that end.

You can't have a war without a buildup of troops.

You can't have a peace without strength.

You can't have prosperity without hard work.

You can't have liberty without weakness.

You can't have the Grace of God without justice for all.

Everyone wants all the blessings that this world has to offer: liberty, security, freedom from want, a life full of potential. Everything that everyone wants can be found in America.

When America plays
She doesn't play
To not lose.
She plays to win.

America certainly has produced her share of great players during her brief time on the world political stage. She undoubtedly will produce more great players in the years to come, and she doesn't plan to ever exit the stage.

In some ways the American Dream doesn't depend on dreams. It depends on facing reality, thinking clearly, working hard, spending, saving, and investing. The American Dream may be our birthright. Achieving it is hard work.

When you think about it you realize it's not the places and things that make America what she is. It is the people, the Americans, and their way of life that make America what she is.

Some of the bad in this world comes from America. Richard Speck, for example, the man who killed eight nurses in 1966, comes to my mind. There are others. But most of the good in this world also comes from America, and that no one can deny.

No one can laugh about America like Americans can.

America imparts to all Americans what they need, and she makes them complete.

What do Americans dislike? Injustice.

What do Americans hold most dear? Liberty, the land on which they live, owner-ship, opportunity—in short, America.

To Americans, life in America is wealth.

To what do Americans adhere? The American Way.

When America prevails in the world, the whole world benefits. When America is disregarded in the world, America doesn't suffer; the world does.

The farther one goes
Away from home
The more he knows
How much he loves
America.

He who devotes himself to America finds that America devotes herself to him.

Americans are always busy doing something, otherwise things would never get done, and there certainly is a lot to be done. This is in contrast to adherents of the Tao, who often advocate doing nothing. Doing nothing is sometimes the right thing to do, but not as often as doing something.

The mind of America is as varied as are the origins and accents of her people, perhaps more so. Sometimes it seems that everyone disagrees about everything. One thing, however, that everyone agrees on: it's great to be an American.

Those who are good to America find that America is good to them. Those who are bad to America? Well, you don't want to find out what happens to those who are bad to America.

America is a place
Of hopes and dreams
And work and joy
And strength and having
And giving and growing
And reaching
Ever higher.
America is a place
Of life.

The light of Liberty
Shines warm and bright
In the hearts
Of all Americans,
No matter where they are,
No matter how they are,
No matter when they are.

The highways of
America
Are straight and fast,
But the byways
Are better by far.
On the byways
You can stop,
Have a long
Look around.
That's where
America
Really is found.

The fields of America are fertile and vast.
Her warehouses are always full.
Her workers always have something to do.
Her people share in the bounty that accrues.

When a man has a job, not only does he benefit, but so does everyone else: in the family, in the neighborhood, in the city, in the state, and in America as well.

America is the biggest, strongest fish in the pond, and the nicest one too.

America has many virtues, among the greatest of which is that, if most people were given the choice, they would rather be here than any other place in the world.

In America, the journey of a thousand miles begins when you fill up with gas and get in the car.

America has a great deal of experience operating a free country. In America, everyone is equal. An American can do or become anything he or she wants to do or become.

America has been blessed to have leaders who loved America more than they loved themselves.

In some ways America values the personal quality of conformity.
In other ways she respects the personal quality of non-conformity.

Our brave young men and women in uniform give their very lives in service to America. If this is the ultimate in self-sacrifice, which it is, it becomes the ultimate debt our country owes, and deserves the ultimate honors she can bestow.

America's
Sincere devotion
To freedom
And justice
Can never be
In doubt.

America has always been,
And ever will be,
Strong,
Because she has always had,
And ever will have,
Right on her side.

It is the Way of Heaven to always be on the side of good, and Heaven is on America's side.

America produces all kinds of Americans. She nourishes them, brings them to their full growth, nurses them, completes them, matures them, maintains them, and overspreads them all. We belong to America, and America belongs to us.

What do Americans
Hold most dear?
The American way.
That says it all.

So there you have *The Tao of America*. Much more could have been said. In fact, the number of things that could be said about America is only limited by the number of Americans you ask. They all have opinions. This book expresses some of mine. The reader can agree with me, disagree, or add to what I have said. But one point upon which there can be no disagreement: it's great to be an American.

Epilogue

And there you have *The Tao of Politics Anthology*. I hope reading it has stimulated your thinking, and I hope that as a result you will find more opportunities to express your opinions as I have expressed mine. Write letters to newspaper editors. Join me at The Tao of Politics (http://taoofpolitics.blogspot.com) for more reading and discussing. Visit other blogs, or start your own blog. Everyone has a right, even a duty, I think, to express his or her own opinions. The world will be a better place if we do.

978-0-595-38473-0
0-595-38473-0

www.ingramcontent.com/pod-product-compliance
Lightning Source LLC
Chambersburg PA
CBHW030311290526
45785CB00001B/304